Hacking

Learning to Hack. Cyber Terrorism, Kali Linux, Computer Hacking, Pen-Testing, & Basic Security.

Seth McKinnon

TABLE OF CONTENTS

Introduction

Hacking is an often-misunderstood skill. We hear so much about it in the media and it oftentimes strikes fear into those who lack knowledge on the topic. You have purchased the book to expand your knowledge in hacking and there could be many reasons for this. Perhaps you would like to learn a little more on how you are able to better protect yourself and your information, maybe you own a small business and have confidential data that you cannot risk being exposed, perhaps you would just like to learn more about hacking to expand your own skills and even find a career within IT security? All of these reasons are great curiosities for picking up this book and we will explore each and every one of them plus more.

Before going any further into the subject of hacking, it is important to clear up the definition of the word as well as what is meant by the term ethical hacking. Too many times do we hear about hacking in the media only to discover that the firm we work for is now hiring someone with hacking skills, how can this be? This will be the topic we explore deeper in the first chapter. From there we will then take a look into the various types of hackers, what their objectives are and what motivates them. This provide you with information that will assist you in understanding the rest of the book as we will then take a deeper look into the techniques and tactics employed by hackers, each with different missions and motives.

There will be a specific focus on penetration testing methods employed ethical hackers to allow you to understand what is meant by this term as well as how organizations are able to use it to better protect themselves. Following from there we will take a detailed look into the career side of hacking as an ethical hacker, what these people do in organizations and also the qualifications which you can obtain to further your career in hacking.

On the other side of the spectrum, we will also take a detailed look into the world of cyber terrorism, what do these people have in common, what motivates them and what are the methods they employ to achieve their objectives. We also take a detailed look into the steps an organization can take in order to protect themselves from cyber terrorist threats and to minimise the damage caused in the event of an attack.

In the final chapter of the book, we will also walk through a simple pentest and software that you can use today in order to get started in hacking. This is performed in a lab like scenario on a virtual machine, allowing you to get a detailed look into how it is done. From this book, we would like to inspire you and grow your curiosity of hacking in the hope that you will further your skills and maybe even explore a career in ethical hacking.

Chapter One: Ethics of Hacking

To those unfamiliar with the concept of hacking, the term can create a myriad of images ranging from dangerous computer criminals to large networks stealing government information. The reason behind this that there is a lot of misconceptions of hacking that portrayed by the media and for people who have a limited knowledge of hacking as an activity. The culture of hacking often times only reaches the mainstream media under circumstances that are unethical, dangerous or when the general public is placed at risk. As a whole, hacking has existed in its current form around the 1960s and has advanced as technology progressed into what we understand to be hacking today.

This begs the question, can hacking be used for ethical reasons and if so what area of society can benefit from skilled hackers, does this put anyone else at risk? This chapter aims to explore these questions and clear up some of the general misconceptions that have placed hackers in a poor light.

What is an Ethical Hacker

An ethical hacker is one which is legally permitted to break into systems in contrast to a hacker that is illegally accessing systems and information without permission and for unethical reasons such as to steal information, to damage systems or for their own entertainment. Ethical hackers are known as "white hat hackers" as opposed to unethical hackers, the "black hatters". There is a group of hackers that rest in between this black and white who are identified as "grey hat hackers" which are known to push the boundaries of ethics and may not always follow the law however their reasons for doing so may be for the greater good of a person or company.

Ethical hackers exist in a profession of their own which has grown dramatically over the years as technology and computing has developed. Ethical hackers may find employment in major corporations involved in technology such as Facebook, Google and Apple as well as performing work for law enforcement agencies to assist them in combating computer crimes.

Improving Security

Our computer networks place an incredible emphasis of security, privacy and protection. The reason for this is that much of what we do online involves exchanging information regarding our personal details and financial documents which if found in the wrong hand can put both our identity and financial security at risk and this is just at the personal level within the home. Corporations and institutions are placed at a much greater risk when exchanging information and holding such information on databases and the demand for such information from criminal organisations, competitors, scammers and thieves is much higher, furthering the need for a heightened security system to secure the passage of this information.

This is where an ethical hacker can provide value to a corporation or organization. Once systems have been established, a hacker can be employed or contracted to discover weaknesses in the system and exploit them to determine how vulnerable the security system is. This is often part of a scientific method to ensure that the systems security capabilities are up to the standard of the corporation seeing if the hacker can access the vital information, they can then detail exactly how this can be done and expose areas of the system which will need to be improved upon.

Weak points can often come about through improper system configurations as well as flaws built into the hardware and software.

4

Hackers are then tasked with researching, identifying, documenting and then relaying any security issues back to the management and IT teams for further improvement. Businesses are then able to refocus their efforts in their security systems to further prevent, eliminate or minimise the probability of further attacks.

Ethical hackers may also take on consulting roles with organizations in order to assist them improving their security measures throughout the corporation, providing feedback, assessment and analysis on their findings.

Developing Products and Services

Hackers are mainly concerned with the coding of software. As there is a greater number of software being published now than ever before, hackers have become an integral part of the business environment. Using their skills in an ethical sense means that hackers are able to assess the security of software products and services used and sold by companies to determine whether these products have weaknesses that could be exploited or flaws in their operation.

This means that many large-scale software publishers also have their own team of hackers providing feedback and information consistently through the development process to ensure that the product or service has been thoroughly assessed on its security capabilities before releasing to the general public to avoid any damage or threat to their personal security and information.

Within an Organization

Hackers are not only limited to coding and behind the scenes security assessment with some taking an active role in an organisation, engaging in social engaging assignments such as searching through the recycling of an organization in the event that valuable information may have been left exposed such as passwords, charts, memos and sticky notes that contain information that would prove valuable in the wrong hands. For this reason, many businesses insist that their employees dispose of documents by shredding to avoid attacks. Through the use of hackers, businesses are able to determine whether employees are following this policy and also demonstrates the consequences if policy and procedure is overlooked.

Ethical hackers may also be employed in a more covert sense, gaining access to employee's information through confidence tricks and shoulder surfing to test the security of a business even within their own office. Through these methods they are able to obtain employee information such as passwords and gain access to systems using these methods, exploiting over thrusting employees. It is this type of work that has placed hackers at the centre of security assessments within organizations as they prove their skill to be very valuable particularly in today's society of reliance on cyberspace as a means of exchanging information.

Chapter Two: Types of Hackers & Their Motivations

There are many types of hackers, each having their own motivations for engaging in the activity. Hacking culture has divided hackers into specific groups or types, identifiable by their knowledge of the culture, their skill, their motivations and their attitudes. Hackers range from many different ages with some being as young as their pre-teens all the way up to older pioneers of the activity. They are found across the world and are only limited by their own potential to learn as well as their access to the cyberspace.

The range of motivations expressed by hackers can vary in ethics, purpose and benefits to them personally as well as society as a whole or even their own employers. When we hear of hackers in the media, we generally have an idea in mind of what this person would look like, they are generally portrayed as being unethical and nefarious however this is represented of just one area or type of hacker which will explore in this chapter. You will soon discover that hackers have motivations that stretch from criminal greed to benefiting society or a group of people and even just for recreation and enjoyment, without causing any harm.

White Hat

White hat hackers are what we had earlier referred to as ethical hackers. White hat hackers work for the greater good of society, corporations and government institutions by using their skill in hacking to test security systems through penetration tests and vulnerability assessments for their client. They also explore the security implications of software products and services. White hat hackers employ a number of tactics to test the viability of security systems with their reward being monetary in the form of a salary, contract, bounty or wages. They also have the satisfaction that they are using their skills in an ethical way, preventing the breakdown of security barriers which protect the personal information of everyday people as well as corporate information that could prove valuable in the wrong hands.

White hat hackers are able to obtain qualification as a Certified Ethical Hacker to allow them to be employed for assessing the security of computer systems. The certification is designed for United States Government agencies and is available only to members of selected agencies. The certification has attracted controversy, from its inception largely due to the methods of testing as well as the stigma that is attached to the definition of hacker which is synonymous with computer crime with some arguing that the field of hackers is largely comprised of criminals and that ethical hacking is grey area that can be contradictory. The certification involves attending training at a centre or through self-study and relevant information security training. From there students will then take an exam involving multiple choice questions within a time limit. The course has changed over the years to reflect the dynamic information security environment.

White hackers can be seen as the good guys whereas the next type of hacker, the blackhat is seen as the stereotypical bad guy, the antagonist in hacking culture.

Black Hat

The black hat hackers are those that are engaging in hacking for the opposite reasons as the white hat hackers. Black hat hackers are mainly concerned with breaking the law to obtain information for personal gain as well as to attack a particular organization or individual. Black hat hackers are often portrayed within the media due to their exploits. Oftentimes they have no legitimate employment other than working within hacker groups for the purpose of illegal gains and attacks. Black hat hackers are seen as typical computer criminals and are the primary antagonist of the white hacker who is actively employed to prevent attacks and access to systems by the black hackers.

Their objectives may be concerned with stealing data for financial gain, destroying or modifying systems to corrupt data or even rendering an entire network unusable for legitimate users. Black hat hackers are responsible for creating viruses that are spread throughout networks and across the internet to succeed in their personal objectives, whatever they may be.

Black hat hackers typically have no formal training other than through their own self-study or mentored by more senior advanced hackers. They are interested in the hacking culture and creating their own code to be used to fulfil their objectives as opposed to hackers that rely on pre-created codes created by other hackers, this group is known as script kiddies.

Grey Hat

As we mentioned in the previous chapter, hacking isn't necessarily black and white, with a group of hackers falling between the lines, known as the grey hat hacker. Grey hats don't operate by any code of ethics; however, their intentions aren't always malicious or for personal gain. A grey hat hacker may use their hacking skills to access a system for recreation or curiosity to see if a particular system can be hacked. From there they may even bring this to the attention of the system administration to alert them of the flaw in their system. They could even take this opportunity to charge a fee to the administration to correct the security flaw.

This is not always the case, with some grey hat hackers accessing systems through security flaws that they later sell to black hat hackers to exploit themselves while profiting this way. While they are not necessarily causing damage or stealing data, they are still profiting from their exploits engaging in unethical behaviour.

The activity of grey hat hackers can still be considered illegal as it breaks laws regarding the accessing of private systems and information without permission and it certainly borders around unethical behaviour, however their motivations are vastly different from the black hat hackers, placing them in a category of their own.

Script Kiddie

The script kiddie is known by a number of names such as skid or skiddie. These are inexperienced hackers who have no true interest in the skill of a hacker, instead rely on codes that have been created by others and use it for malicious activities. They generally carry out activities for their own entertainment or out of curiosity, downloading and copying code or software to create a virus which they will then use to target someone that might know or an organization they feel like taking revenge on. They generally learn and pick up skill as they progress, taking advantage of online tutorials and videos to practice using the software they have obtained.

The script kiddies often use attacks such as Denial of Service and Distributed Denial of Service (DoSing or DDoSing) which causes a system to crash due to an overwhelming influx of information. The name comes from the common association that many of these hackers are quite young and inexperienced, relying on scripts or tools that others have created to carry out their activities, showing no interest in creating their own code, tools or software.

Neophyte

The neophyte also has a number of associated names such as newbie, noob or green hat. The difference between the Neophyte and the Script Kiddie is that the neophytes show an interest in learning the skill of hacking and are looking to expand their knowledge base and their capabilities to expand their arsenal and grow their skills in hacking. The neophyte is the starting point for both black, white and grey hat hackers and their placement in these cliques is determined by their motivations for engaging in hacking.

The neophytes will source their knowledge from other hackers in the community as well tutorials and videos found online. Their lack of knowledge and experience is what gives them their name but as they begin to learn and take advantage of new found knowledge, they progress further to being a recognised hacker.

Elite Hacker

At the opposite end of the spectrum from the Neophyte and Script Kiddies, is the Elite Hacker. The Elite Hackers are very well recognised within the community achieving a social status among other hackers. The elite hacker has a considerable level of skill and experience and often times they are the first to discover new exploits before distributing it throughout the community.

Elite hackers can also fit into any category such as black hat, white hat and grey hat depending on their motivations and how they put their skills to use.

Red Hat

Red hat hackers are similar in the operations of white hat hackers although far more extreme. They are known as the vigilantes of the hacker world, taking an ethical approach to their actions however approaching it in a controversial way. For example, if they discover that a black hat hacker has exploited a defect and don't agree with the operations of that particular hacker, they will seek vengeance using much of the same methods. Rather than reporting the defect or the hacker, the red hat hacker will attack the black hat hacker through using viruses, DoSing as well as accessing their private information and destroying their system significantly. The red hat hacker operates as though they must put a stop to the unethical hackers themselves rather than simply strengthening the security of the system that had been attacked or informing authorities.

Hacktivist

In recent years, the concept of the Hacktivist has emerged, finding attention in the mainstream media for their efforts. The hacktivist is a hacker that utilizes their skills and technology to deliver and publicize a message of a political, social, ideological or a religious agenda. These types of hackers may also fall into a number of categories such as grey hat or red hat depending on their motivations as you now may start to understand.

As a whole, hacktivism can be divided into two distinct groups. There are hackers that engage in what is known as cyber terrorism which involves launching attacks with an agenda, defacing a website or DoSing to achieve their desired result. We will explore cyberterrorism further in a later chapter as it is quite an in-depth subject. These hackers will fall more towards the black and red hat style of hacking in that their objectives are more sinister and menacing, although still acting in a way that they feel is for the greater good, yet still quite illegal and damaging to their targets. An example of a highly recognised hacktivist group that engages in methods of cyberterrorism is that the group 'Anonymous' which claims to fight for justice against wrongdoers across the globe. The group is comprised of a loose network of hackers with a decentralized command structures, claiming to operate on ideas rather than directives.

The other element of hacktivism is those that engage in releasing information freely to the public as a means of exposing corruption and unethical behaviour by corporations, organizations and even individuals. There have been some high-profile examples of these individuals in recent years such as the infamous Julian Assange, responsible for the creation and publication of WikiLeaks. The non-profit organization was dedicated to published secret information and classified documents to the public.

Organized Crime

At the opposite end of the spectrum from hacktivists is the organized criminal gangs comprised of black hat hackers. These groups of hackers are mainly concerned with profit maximising through their activities which often involve stealing data from banks and corporations. These types of hackers are those that are most feared in mainstream society due to the damage that can be done and the high level of resources in place to ensure that they are neutralized or the harm is kept to a minimum.

Nation States

Finally, there is the nation state. This group involves qualified hackers employed by intelligence on behalf of governments to engage in cyberwarfare internationally. This generally involves causing damage to a rival nations security network or performing espionage to obtain data that will provide insights into a country's military information. Governments may also employ hackers to protect their networks from attacks and spies infiltrating the system. There have been a number of incidents in recent years involving governments suffering highly publicized attacks occurring in cyberwarfare. It can be difficult to determine the origin of such attacks and therefore can be an effective means of both sabotage and espionage.

Chapter Three: Hacking Techniques & Tactics

Having an understanding of the techniques used by hackers to not only access your information without permission will allow you to gain insight into how this is possible as well as what you are able to do to protect yourself from the most basic of attacks. Using this knowledge, you are also able to explore further in hacking if you wish to develop your skills and discover additional knowledge into creating your own programs and software.

Keylogger

A keylogger is a very simple piece of software that is designed to track and record each keystroke made by the user of computer. These keystrokes and sequences are then stored on a log file that is accessed by the hacker who is able to discern your information such as email ID's, passwords, banking details, credit card numbers and virtually anything else that you input into your machine using the keyboard. For this reason, many online banking sites and other highly secure web pages use virtual keyboards and even image identifying passcodes to provide you with access to your account since these cannot be recorded through keyloggers.

How do you keyloggers gain access to your computer in the first place? These lines of code or software are often attached to files that are downloaded onto your computer without you being aware, known as Trojans (deriving from the Greek mythology of the Trojan Horse). These files then get to work are report back to the hacker with the information collecting from your computer. Other ways that these files are able to access your computer is if they are placed on the computer either through direct access, if someone was to have access to your computer with permission to allow them to place the file on the computer or through USB drives that they have provided to you with hidden files rooted within.

Keyloggers may also find themselves used in white hat purposes such as within organizations to ensure that employees are following the correct policies and procedures and not engaging in deceptive conduct.

Denial of Service (DoS/DDoS)

One of the most common forms of hacking attacks is the Denial of Service, as we had mentioned earlier. This involves causing a website to become unusable. The site is taken down due to the flooding of information and traffic, enough to overload the system as it struggles to process all the requests and is ultimately overwhelmed and crashes. These attacks are employed by hackers who aim to disrupt websites or servers that they want to cause destruction to for whatever their reason or motivation was. For example, a hacktivist hacker might take down a website that disagrees with their political views seeing it as their moral duty. Whereas a black hat hacker might take down the website of a competing organization to disrupt their services and sabotage the efforts of their competitor.

A DoS attack is carried out using tools such as botnets or a network of infected systems which are then used almost as an army of zombified servers to repeatedly attack the target service, overloading it. These infected systems are created through emails and software which carry a virus and once infected, these zombie computers are able to be used at will by the hackers. It has been revealed through industry data that up to 45% of organizations suffer from DDoS attacks resulting in millions of dollars worth of damage each year.

Vulnerability Scanner

To detect weaknesses within a computer network, hackers use a tool known as vulnerability scanner. This could also refer to port scanners which are used to scan a specific computer for available access points that the hacker would be able to take advantage of. The port scanner is also able to determine what programs or processes are running on that particular port which allows hackers to gain other useful information. Firewalls have been created to prevent unauthorised access to these ports however this is more of a harm reduction strategy rather than a sure-fire way to prevent hackers.

Some hackers are able to discern access points manually rather than using a program. This involves reading the code of a computer system and testing weaknesses to see if they are able to obtain access. They can also employ methods of reverse engineering the program to recreate the code if they are unable to view the code.

Brute Force Attack

If you have ever wondered why you have a limited number chances to enter your password before being denied access, the server you are attempting to access has a safeguard against brute force attack. Brute force attack involves software that attempts to recreate the password by scanning through a dictionary or random word generator in an extremely short amount of time to hit on the password and gain access. For this reason, passwords have advanced to become far longer and more complex than they once were in the past, such as including characters, numbers, upper and lower-case letters and some going as far as barring words that are found in the dictionary.

Waterhole Attacks

Waterhole attacks are known by this name due to the fact hackers prey on physical locations where a high number of people will access their computers and exchange secure information. Similar in a way that a waterhole can be poisoned for the wildlife surrounding, the hacker can poison a physical access point to claim a victim. For example, a hacker may use a physical point such as a coffee shop, coworking space or a public Wi-Fi access point. These hackers are then able to track your activity, websites frequented and the times that you will be accessing your information and strategically redirect your path to a false webpage that allows the information to be sent through to the hacker and allow them to use it at a later time at their leisure. Be sure that when you are using public Wi-Fi, you have appropriate anti spyware and antivirus software to alert you when there may be suspicious activity while online.

False WAP

Similarly, to the waterhole attack, the hacker can create, using software, a fake wireless access point. The WAP is connected to the official public wireless access point however once the victim connects they are exposed and vulnerable in that their data can be accessed at any point and stolen. When in public spaces, ensure that the WAP you are using is the correct one, they will generally have a password prior to access or a portal which will require you to enter a username, email address and password which is obtained from the administer. If you find the access point is completely open, this could be a cause for alarm knowing that this point is likely bait.

Phishing

Another common technique used by hackers to obtain secure information from an unsuspecting victim is through phishing. Phishing involves a hacker creating a link that you would normally associate with a site that you commonly access such as a banking site or payment portal. However, when you input your details, they are sent to the hacker rather than the institution that you you believe you are sending them to. Phishing is often times done through sending false emails that appear as though they are from your bank or billing institution and generally request that you access your account to either update your details or make a payment.

There are ways to distinguish whether you are being targeted for phishing such as checking the sender's ID (which can still be falsified) or checking the details of the link that you have been provided and seeing that it doesn't match up with the usual site that you fill your details in. You may also notice formatting issues with the email such as logos out of place or poor formatting that would indicate that the phisher is not using the correct template. Many institutions will insist that they would not request your details through email or ask you to update your details and if you do receive your bill through email, if you feel suspicious you can check with previous billing emails or even call your institution to double check that the email is genuine.

Clickjacking Attacks

If you have ever attempted to stream a video on a less reputable site, you may have noticed that the interface can be quite confusing to navigate due to false play buttons or common sections after which you click on them and are then redirected somewhere else. These are known as Clickjacking attacks as well as UI Redress. While redirecting to the ad or another page may seem harmless, when done correctly these attacks can be quite sinister and potentially dangerous as they are able to capture your information. You need to exercise extra caution when using unfamiliar websites as they may not be as safe as they appear, with their interface taking you to a place right where the hacker wants you. Always be aware of the URL of each click you make and if it differs drastically from the website that you were just on, ensure that where you are taken does not involve any downloads or exchanging of details for your own protection.

Bait and Switch

The bait and switch technique involves the hacker supplying you with a program that appears to be authentic but when it faces it is a virus or a tool used by the hacker to access your computer. These can generally be found in unscrupulous websites that offer pirated programs, software, movies or games that are in high demand. Once you download the program, you will find that the file is not what you had intended and instead had loaded a virus to your computer to provide the hacker with access.

Social Engineering

We mentioned earlier, the social engineering techniques used by white hat hackers. This technique is often overlooked as a means of hacking however it can be quite effective. An example of social engineering is conning a system administrator into supplying details by posing as a user or an individual with legitimate access. These hackers are often thought of as con men rather than what we understand to be hackers, however it is a means of hacking nonetheless. Many of these hackers have a good understanding of the security practices of the organization in which are attacking. They will target and prey on those who may not be as experienced or with a lower level security clearance than some of the higher ups. For example, they may phone up the employee on the helpdesk and request access to the system and without the experience to understand the consequences of providing information to an unknown source, give it up. There are a number of categories that social engineering can be placed in, these being:

Intimidation - An example of intimidation would involve a superior such as a manager or supervisor calling the help desk technician, angry and threatening to punish the technician if their authority is questioned. Under pressure, the employee will comply and provide the information. Their questioning of the authority is promptly shut down as the employee values their job and offers to assist the hacker in securing the information.

Helpfulness - On the opposite end of the spectrum, there is the helpfulness technique. This involves feigning distress and concern to take advantage of a technician's nature to offer help and compassion. Rather than acting angry and placing pressure on the technician, the distressed hacker will act as though they themselves are under pressure and worrisome of the outcome. The technician will provide assistance in any way they can regardless of considering the consequences at the risk of causing further distress to the hacker.

Name-dropping - Having the name of an authorised user provides the hacker with the advantage that they can pretend to be a specific person who should rightly have access to the information. This can be done by sourcing through web pages of companies which can be easily found online. Another example of this is the searching through documents that have been improperly discarded, providing vital details to the hacker.

Technical - The other area of social engineering hacking is using technology as a means of support to obtain information. This can involve a hacker sending a fax or an email to a legitimate user which requires the user to respond with sensitive information. The hacker often poses as law information or a legal representative, requiring the information as part of an ongoing investigation for their files.

Rootkit

A rootkit finds its way onto your operating system through legitimate processes, using low-level and hard to detect program. The rootkit can assume control of the operating system from the user and since the program itself is hidden within the system binaries as replacement pieces of code, it can be incredibly difficult and virtually impossible for the user to detect and remove the program manually.

Packet Analyser

When transmitting data across the internet or any other network, an application known as a packet analyser or packet sniffer can be used by a hacker to capture data packets which may contain critical information such as passwords and other records.

Chapter Four: Penetration Testing

Penetration testing is a simulated attack on a computer system, network or server that analyses and assess vulnerabilities and weaknesses within the system security and once identified the hacker is able to gain access to the features on the system and steal the data.

The process is designed to identify a target system and is approached with a specific goal in mind. The test will then gather data and analyse the information presented to it and determine the most viable option to achieve the chosen objective.

There are two distinct targets which a penetration test will be directed towards. These are white box and black box. The white box target is one which provides a breakdown of the background and system information whereas the black box supplies nothing other than the company name. The main mission of the penetration test is to assess the weaknesses within the system's defences and vulnerabilities which could be exploited. The test will provide details of which areas of the system's defences have failed and supply this information as a means of improving these areas. This data is then sent back through to the system administration who will then use the reports compiled by the penetration test to determine a course of action and how the organization can implement countermeasures to avoid future attacks, exploiting these vulnerabilities.

There are many goals associated with penetration testing which we'll go into further detail on throughout this chapter. The goal is largely dependent on the organization and their requirements for their system. The penetration test is also broken down into five phases which will also cover in greater detail for each phase. These phases are Reconnaissance, Scanning, Gaining Access, Maintaining

Access and Covering Tracks. Penetration tests are available through a number of tools some of which are supplied operating systems as well as free software depending on the uses for each one, whether in a commercial or domestic sense.

Phases One: Reconnaissance

Before one undertakes a penetration test, they must first enter the reconnaissance phase or the discovery phase. This involves collecting preliminary data on the target in question and how it operates. This phase is generally the longest of the five and can take as long as a few weeks or even months. Data is collected by a number of means and the lengths that hacker goes to in order to obtain data will depend upon the backers own objectives and whether they are working in an ethical white hat sense or if their means of attack is that of a black hat.

The data collected can come through methods such as:

- Internet searching

- Social Engineering Techniques

- Dumpster Diving

- Domain name management/search services

- Non-Intrusive network scanning

For an organization to defend against a hacker in the reconnaissance phase they will need to go to great lengths as it can be quite difficult. This is because most organizations will have some degree of public presence or their information can be found across the internet in some form. As we mentioned before the method for obtaining data can be as simple as social engineering in which the hacker is able to coerce employees to provide information. This could even happen over a long period of time in which the hacker continuously sources small pieces of information from employees and overtime they are able to complete the puzzle and discover opportunities where there are security weaknesses and vulnerabilities that can be exploited.

This isn't to say there aren't things an organization can do to protect themselves from this type of hacking. For example, certain pieces of information can be kept confidential such as version numbers and patch levels of certain software, email addresses should be hidden from public view on websites as well as the names and positions of key personnel and where they stand in the overall company structure in relation to other members of staff.

Training can be undertaken to ensure staff members follow the correct protocol when dealing with confidential data such as destroying documents that have printed information rather than simply tossing it in the recycling or garage. They should also be warned when communicating with people they are unfamiliar with and avoid providing any information without proper clearance. This can be done through white hat methods, with hackers simulating an attack to ensure that employees are assessed in their handling of confidential information.

In terms of online information, contact information and domain name registration lookups should be generic and network devices should be protected from scanning attempts.

By taking these precautions, the organization can have a less likely chance that a hacker will be able to access the information required for an attack. This doesn't mean they won't attempt or continue to pressure the organization to gain access and there is still a chance that they can ultimately obtain access, it does however make the job much harder for them and have a higher probability of being caught.

Phase 2: Scanning

The hacker takes the information that has been collected during reconnaissance phase and from there assesses the data that has been compiled. From this, they are able to have an understanding of how the business operates and the value of the information that can be access during the attack.

Once the attack weighs up the value of the data that can be accessed from their assessment of data collected they move through to the scanning phase. The scanning phase involves scanning the perimeter and internal network comprised of all devices and seeks to discover a weakness that can be exploited. These weaknesses can be found in open ports that are being unused, open services that can be hijacked, applications that have poor protection or are vulnerable which can also be operating systems without adequate security capabilities, data that is being transmitted that lacks the proper protection as well as the make and model information for each piece of LAN/WAN equipment.

There are ways in which scans can be detected such as through Intrusion Detection Solutions (IDS) or Intrusion Prevention Solutions (IPS) however these are not always effective as hackers are continually advancing and creating new circumnavigational techniques to avoid such controls. As hackers advance their techniques and tools, so too do the tools of security services, providing protection to the systems that are used by organizations. This is done through patches and releases of preventative solutions therefore it is best to consistently update software and security tools to ensure you have protection in the latest advances of black hat hackers.

There are some methods which system administrators can employ to ensure there is a reduced risk of an attack occurring or scans being performed on the system. For example, an administrator could shut down all ports that are no longer being used and close down any services that could be hijacked. Critical devices which are used for processing sensitive information should be set to only respond to devices which have been approved to avoid external devices taking advantage of their freedom of use.

Another method for reducing the chances of a scan is to assess the system design and secure any services by resisting any attempts for external access. This allows you to have a say in who is to access the server and when in a controlled environment. Another preventative measure you can perform is to maintain proper patch levels on endpoint and LAN/WAN systems.

Scanning is performed using a number of tools and applications on the behalf of the hacker. We will have a further look into the tools used in penetration testing further along in this chapter. Scanning is similar to the reconnaissance phase however it is at a more targeted level, scanning the target that is to be attacked whereas the reconnaissance phase is directed more towards the organization. Once the hacker has secured an even more defined target, the entry point, they are to move onto the next phase. Gaining Access.

Phase 3: Gaining Access

This the climax of the penetration attack. The hacker now has access to the resources available on the database of the organization. The hacker is then free to either extract the information that he sees of value or he is able to take control of the network and use it as a base to launch further attacks against other targeted networks in how we described a DoS attack. By gaining access to the network, the hacker now has control over one or more devices.

As was the case in the preventative measures of scanning, there are some precautions that administrators and security personnel are able to take to ensure that devices and services are more challenging to access by legitimate users such as black hat hackers. This can involve restricting access of users such who have no legitimate day to day requirement to be accessing the devices. Furthermore, security managers should be closely monitoring the domains and those who are accessing services such as local administrators. Using physical security controls will allow managers to detect attacks that are occurring in real time and can deny access while also alerting the proper authorities to ensure the intruder is exposed.

Another approach which can be taken to ensure that access is denied is to encrypt highly sensitive and confidential information using protection keys. This would mean that any attacker attempting to access the system regardless of how well the system is protected, will gain access only to find that the information is scrambled and with the keys protected, the attacker would have no reliable method for using the data that has been encrypted. Encryption is a good final line of defence for particularly valuable data however it cannot be relied upon entirely in itself. Even if the attacker was to access the system and discover that the data is encrypted, they can still wreak havoc on the network and even disable it, causing significant damage as a means of sabotage. Even more alarming, the attacker could have control over the system and use it for further crimes which could be traced back to the organization's network.

Once the attack has gained access to the system, they are still far from being in the clear. Access is for a limited time, the longer the hacker is operating from the system, the greater the chances of being caught. The hacker must then shift to the next phase, maintaining access to ensure they are able to collect as much data as possible.

Maintaining Access

The hacker is working against the clock at this point and they must ensure they are able to maintain access long enough to succeed in what they had set out to do whether this was to steal critical data and information or to launch a further attack from the encumbered server. The hacker has been able to avoid detection up until this point, however they are still at risk of being caught and the longer they have access to the system, the higher the risk they could be detected.

While you can make use of both IDS and IPS devices to detect hackers accessing the system, you can also detect when a hacker is departing from the system. This is known as an extrusion and there are a number of method this can be done. The primary way you can identify your system has been in use from an unauthorised assailant is by detecting file transfers to external sites from internal devices. This indicates that data is being transferred from your server and being sent to external source and if this source is unfamiliar, it could indicate theft.

Another method is to detect any sessions which have begun between servers in the internal data centre and external networks that are not under your control. This also includes sessions that have an unusual duration, frequency and amount of content. You can also look for connections to odd ports or nonstandard protocols that indicate an external influence. Identifying an unusual network or server behaviour that is out of the ordinary is a giveaway that there is some unauthorised activity occurring on the network indicative of an intrusion. Assessing the traffic mix per time interval can also indicate that there is external access to the system that is not in line with the regular practices of the business.

Once the hacker has remained in control of the system for long enough to achieve all their objectives, they are then to move onto the next stage which is to both prevent themselves from being caught and exposed as well as establish a basis for re-entry should they need to return.

Phase 5: Covering Tracks

The final step for the hacker to take involves removing any evidence of their intrusion as well as establish controls which can be used at a later time should they need to re access the system. These controls will also need to be hidden and undetectable to avoid their removal. This is obviously the most difficult stage to detect a hacker as they are deliberately removing information that could alert security personnel.

It is still possible at this stage to detect an intruder, however it is likely that your system would have experienced a breach of security and a loss of data as a result of the attack. In this case, the best course of action is to perform a system mind assessment to discover any activity or processes that exist on the system that are not in line with the normal operation of the business. Once you have been alerted of an attacker, even if the hacker has long gone, security protocols should be upgraded to combat future attacks.

You may find it valuable to explore security solutions such as anti-malware, personal firewalls, host based IPS solutions and an improvement on security protocols and training of staff to be able to detect future events themselves and prevent further damage.

Chapter Five: Careers in Hacking

If you feel that hacking is a skill that you are interested in and possibly you have gained experience yourself perhaps in less ethical methods, you may be interested in a career in hacking. As we mentioned earlier, many corporations and institutions often hire white hat hackers in order to improve their security capabilities and keep abreast of all developments in hacker culture.

There has never been a better time to be involved in the IT security field with the Bureau of Labor Statistics estimating that the sector is set to grow approximately 18 percent by 2024. Even more exciting for newcomers to the field is that the demand for skilled hackers is up by 40% according to a survey completed by the Ponemon Institute. This indicates that within the last few years there is roughly 40% of positions going unfulfilled within the IT security field. This could also be an indication that many skilled hackers are not willing to put their skills to use in a legitimate career, creating opportunities for white hat, ethical hackers.

As we mentioned earlier, there are many opportunities being created for ethical hackers to perform penetration tests to determine the viability of a networks security. For the right person, this type of work can be incredibly rewarding with pay exceeding six figures per year. The average security analyst in the United States makes over $96,000 per year.

As we rely increasing on technology and the constant developments in the IT field, the demand and job prospects for IT security professionals will continue to grow as the skills and requirements for hacker's change. As we had mentioned earlier in chapter 1, an ethical hack is tasked with consulting an organization in how they are able to reduce the number of vulnerabilities that could be exploited by black hat hackers and working with developers to advise on how they are able to better address their security requirements. This leads to the updating of security policies and procedures and further training of staff as part of a company's security awareness and training program.

Job Requirements for Hackers

Despite the significant shortage and demand for ethical hackers, there are still requirements for an entry level ethical hacker to find himself a position within the IT security field. As a minimum, most white hat hackers will require a bachelor degree within computer science or a related field to secure an interview within an organization. Further from that the hacker will also require specific security certifications which will demonstrate that the hacker possess the appropriate level of experience and skill to perform the job to the best of their knowledge. Evidence for this has been demonstrated by the SANS Salary & Certification survey of 2008 in which 81% of respondents within the IT security field stated that having certifications was a key factor in securing their positions.

There are three primary security certifications which are recognised within the industry and although there is an abundance of other certifications, these have the greatest value when looking to secure a position. They are:

- Certified Ethical Hacker (CEH)
- GIAC (Global Information Assurance Certification) Penetration Tester (GPEN)
- Offensive Security Certified Professional (OSCP)

Certified Ethical Hacker (CEH)

We had briefly touched on the Certified Ethical Hacker certification earlier in the book in chapter 2, however we will cover it further detail here. The CEH certification is the staple of hackers in the industry and covers a wide variety of topics within the field, being the broadest of all three. The certification is offered by the EC-Council with the main objective of the certification is to provide security professionals a baseline knowledge of security threats, risks and countermeasures to allow them to have the most basic of understandings of what being a hacker entails. The course is delivered through both lectures and practical lab based lessons.

Before enrolling, students should at the very least have a basic understanding of Windows and Linux system administration as well as TCP/IP and virtualization. Classes are not compulsory and students are able to enrol and opt to just take the exams provided they are able to submit proof that they have prior experience within IT security, 2 years to be exact.

The flexibility of the CEH certification is one of the most valued advantages of the course. Students are able to learn through self-study and video lectures which they are able to go through at their own pace and even the instructor led lessons are able to be taken online. If students are already employed with a business or organization in the security field, they are able to bridge their training in conjunction with their work.

The course is broken down over the course of five days, with each day being eight hours long. Students are able to access online labs for six months following their enrolment. As we mentioned earlier, the exam is comprised of 125 multiple choice questions over the course of four hours with a 70% minimum pass threshold to receive certification.

The general knowledge of the course provides students with an all-round experience of what is expected of them in the industry with no specific focus on any software, product, technology or skill. Students are expected to understand how to correctly scan a network to identify basic viruses as well as how to perform penetration testing and how a web server can be hijacked. Another element of the course is the social engineering aspect of hacking, informing hackers how they are able to manipulate and influence individuals to obtain personal and confidential information in order to infiltrate a computer system. In recent years, particularly as human communication has advanced to the point of online messaging and social media, social engineering has become a crucial element of hacking.

The course does have some drawbacks however being incredibly dependant on text and video instruction without too much of a focus on the hands-on practice. It has also been noted by industry experts that the course is somewhat outdated and is too simple for providing enough scope for day to day use. It does however present an excellent overview of the industry and those hackers looking to specialise are welcome to explore further certifications to gain more precise knowledge. The CEH is a more cost-effective certification to gain an insight into the industry and should not be treated as anything comprehensive.

The CEH certification is well known within the IT security field and having the qualification is a significant advantage to have documented on your resume. While it won't make you stand too far out from the crowd of other applicants, the certification will enable you to be on the radar of potential employers being the most recognised certification in the industry.

Network Penetration Tester (GPEN)

For those looking at expanding their skills in network penetration testing, the GPEN is the course to take you much deeper into this particular field of knowledge. The course takes students through what is involved in a penetration test before taking the GPEN test to obtain their certification.

Before undertaking a network penetration testing course, students should at the very least have an understanding the different types of cryptography within Windows, Linux and also an understanding of TCP/IP, many courses offer refreshers on these subjects to bring students up to speed but the prior knowledge will help when progressing through the course they are however not set in stone prerequisites.

Throughout the course, students will take part in over 30 labs, getting hands on practical experience through the pen-testing process with everything from detail reconnaissance, scanning and how to write and interpret a penetration testing report for conveying such information to management and technical staff. This will allow students to have a good idea of what is required when performing penetration tests in a corporate environment.

Coursework is generally completed through a Linux distribution containing everything the student will need such as Metasploit tools and free open source software such as password-breaker John the Ripper, taking advantage of some of the most widely used and most advanced tools the industry has to offer.

The course also aims to open students up to the perspective of the hacker when attacking the business, changing the mindset of students to approach the penetration in a way that they are able to think outside of the box and launch the attack in ways that would have been unintended from the point of view of the business.

The costs involved with the course can be a deterrent, particularly for those who are looking to break into the industry, however the practical hands on experience will allow students to present themselves as a cut above the rest and provide themselves with a career boost and a significant raise if they are currently working with the industry. The course can be difficult to get through with a huge amount of information presented over six days. The practical experience however will allow students to refine their skills as an ethical hacker and open new avenues in their career.

The exam consists of 115 multiple choice questions and is open book. The timeframe for the exam is run over three hours with students requiring a 74 percent pass threshold in order to receive the certification. The cost of the course varies whether you decide to take the online option or the in-person training with the latter being more considered once the compulsory online labs are taken into account.

Offensive Security Certified Professional (OSCP)

The OSCP is by far the most technical and specialised certification of the three. The certification is aimed towards providing an in depth and hands on insight into the penetration testing process and lifecycle. The certification aims to steer away from a classroom setting instead opting to be more focused on the practical aspects.

Students are first expected to complete the Penetration Testing with Kali Linux (PWK) course a course which has been built around the Kali Linux Distribution open source project which is maintained by the administers of the course, Offensive Security. Students will need to have a solid understanding of TCP/IP, networking and reasonable Linux skill as a minimum requirement.

The course is offered online with the only live training facility being in Las Vegas, Nevada. The cost of the course is determined by the length you will be accessing the online labs with options for 30 days and 90 days. During this time, you will be provided with video lessons, access to the labs and finally the certification test.

The OSCP is unique in that the test is not performed by multiple choice and instead is performed through a virtual networking in which you are tasked with researching the network, identifying vulnerabilities and then hacking the system to obtain administrative access similar to how a simulation would work. You are then asked to provide a comprehensive penetration test report to detail your findings, creating an environment that would mimic that of a real-world situation. The test is completed over 24 hours with the report being reviewed by a certification committee to obtain a passing grade.

While the OSCP is designed to develop skills focused on pen-testing tools and techniques, the certification also explores more out of the box thinking and unique approaches to solving problems. The test is structured in a way that students learn how to think laterally and that students will be able to not only find and exploit vulnerabilities but also further escalate their privileges and gain experience in scenarios that they may be faced with in the future.

The test is geared more towards advance security personnel in the IT field, with the hands-on approach taking much time with the trial and error approach however, this is incredibly beneficial for those looking to advance in the industry. Students are able to learn from hands on experience rather than just knowledge and are able to put their skills into practice in real scenarios.

There are downsides to the course however with students not being able to speak with a live instructor in the case that they may need to ask questions or may be stuck and require assistance in the labs. The course is also far less recognised than the CEH which can mean that you will not necessarily standout from the field of other applicants as well as you would with a more recognised course. The education however will provide you with a greater understanding of pen-testing, increasing your productivity and performance while at work which is something that cannot be said of other more knowledge based courses.

If a hacker wants to have an in depth understanding of pen-testing and become a specialist in their field, the OSCP will provide that level of experience and skill through the simulation exam, more so than any other course.

Which is the Best Course for You?

Your decision to take on any one of these courses will be founded in having a desire to further develop your knowledge and skills within the topics that are presented. Each one has its own pros and cons within the industry and it is down to the ethical hacker to decide where they are in their career and where they would like to take it. For example, for those who are looking to get started with a shift in their career and hoping to break into the industry, the CEH will provide them with the broad knowledge required and industry recognition for them to be considered for the position, however the information may be outdated and not for those who are looking to specialise or become exceptionally skilled in the industry.

If a student aims to develop their skills further and have a more comprehensive understanding of penetration testing, the GPEN uses tools that are widely used in the industry and allows for one on one instructions. The course also explores the social engineering aspect of hacking which is widely becoming recognised as a very important element of hacking particularly in the age of social media and technology dedicated to communicating, while still lacking high security measures. This can provide a career boost for one who is looking to increase their qualifications and their pay however the course comes at a cost.

Finally, if you are looking to specialise in pen-testing and have an understanding of the entire process the OSCP will provide you with extensive knowledge tested through a simulation scenario and while the course is not recognized as widely as the other courses, you can be sure that your practical experience in the workplace is of the highest standard. The lack of instruction and heavy course load can be overwhelming for beginners and therefore this course is recommended for those who have experience working within the IT security field as opposed to those who are looking to start in the industry.

Chapter Six: Cyber Terrorism

At the opposite end of the spectrum of the ethical hacker is the action of cyberterrorism. Cyberterrorism is defined as using the internet to conduct violent acts that result in or threaten the loss of life or significant bodily harm in order to achieve political gains through intimidation. As computing technology advances, so too does the risk of cyber terrorism on not only personal networks but also of government institutions, banking and security organizations, in which the damage can be quite widespread. Cyberterrorism is largely different from aforementioned cybercrime as the nature of cyber terrorism is more to inflict fear and devastation upon a network and it's the institution it is contained within.

Cyberterrorism can be conducted in order to reach some kind of personal objective through the use of computer networks and the internet with some experienced cyberterrorists being able to cause mass damage towards government systems, hospital records as well as national military and security programs that leave a country in a state of turmoil, terrified of further attacks. The objective for many cyberterrorists is often related to political or ideological agendas.

Cyberterrorism can be challenging to prevent or protect systems from as it can be largely anonymous with unknown motivations and uncertainty over whether there could be repeated attacks again in the future. There is some argument over the exact definitions of cyber terrorism or whether it should be referred to as terrorism at all since the actions are not closely linked with conventional methods of terrorism and instead are towards information warfare, however since many of the motives are political in nature and targeted towards the disruption of infrastructure, the term loosely fits into the category of terrorism.

Cyberterrorism can be committed by individuals, groups and organizations and in some cases by nation states attacking rival governments. Cyberterrorism is currently a major concern for both government and media sources due to the potential damages with government agencies such as the Federal Bureau of Investigations (FBI) and the Central Intelligence Agency establish targeted strike forces to reduce the damage caused by cyber terrorism.

Cyberterrorism can be accomplished through a variety of techniques such as a network penetration and viruses that are created in order to disrupt and immobilize the system. Cyberterrorism is more dangerous than simple cybercrime for personal gain. Cyberterrorism can have serious consequences on the country and institutions that are attacked, placing lives at risk. As our technology improves, there are a number of ways to combat cyberterrorism by first anticipating and preparing for attacks and to implement a plan for prevention, following this we prepare for incident management to mitigate an attack limit the damage caused in the case that an attack has reached the target. Once an attack has occurred, the next stage of defence is to implement consequence management which is assessing the damage and taking note of how we are able to improve defences in the future, starting the process over once again.

Traits of Cyber Terrorism

After understanding the definition of cyber terrorism, many cyber terrorists have found to have very similar traits in common which can place them in the category of cyber terrorists. One such trait is that the victims of cyber terrorist attacks are specifically targeted rather than random in the case of hackers without clear objectives other than financial gain or entertainment. While there can be randomised cases of hackers releasing viruses or worms into the general public, there are often clear objectives for doing so with the victims being a specific group or nation that has been targeted for predetermined reasons by the hacker. Other objectives involve attacking an organization, industry, sector or economy for the purpose of inflicting damage or destroying their target.

Finally, another common trait within cyber terrorism is to further the terrorist group's own goals which could be financial, political, religious or ideological. These terrorists seek to achieve this goal by inflicting heavy damages on their target and make their own objectives obvious by publicising them.

Types of Cyber Terrorism Attack

Cyberterrorism has been placed within three main categories by the Centre for the Study of Terrorism and Irregular Warfare at the Naval Postgraduate school in Monterey, California. These categories are simple-unstructured, advanced-structured and complex-coordinated.

Simple-Unstructured - These are small-scale attacks and are generally performed by inexperienced hackers using widely available tools created by other people. The hackers behind these kinds of attacks generally lack command and control skills as well as possessing a limited learning capability.

Advanced-Structured - These types of attacks are more sophisticated and can target multiple systems or networks and the hackers responsible possess the capability to modify or even create basic hacking tools. While the hackers possess limited command and control skills, they have an increase learning capability and present a significant risk depending on the organization they are targeting.

Complex-Coordinated - At the higher end the scale, coordinated and complex attacks can have a devastating effect on the system under attack with mass disruptions against integrated and heterogeneous defences. These types of hackers have the ability to create sophisticated hacking tools and have a strong command and control as well as an advanced capacity for further learning and skill development.

The types of attacks that can occur are incursion, destruction, disinformation, denial of service and defacement of websites. Each of these has a varying level of sophistication and devastation and largely depend on the motivation and objectives of the hackers. Understanding each type of attack allows organizations to develop the proper counter measures to combat and prevent an attack as well as implement damage control in the wake of an attack.

Incursion - The objective of an incursion attack is to gain access or penetrate the networks and systems which contain valuable information for the attacks. This is one of the more common attacks and has a much greater success rates for the terrorists. Due to the high number of loopholes available to hackers, terrorists are able to take advantage of weak security and vulnerabilities to obtain or even modify secure information which can then be recycled for further attacks against the organization or for the personal gain of the attackers.

Destruction - This is a far more severe attack with the objective to infiltrate a computer system and inflict damage and ultimately destroy the network. For the organizations who are victim to these types of attacks, there can be incredible costs involved both in terms of repair and loss of revenue. At the most extreme end of the scale an attacker intent on destruction can render an organization inoperable with their entire system thrown into disarray, impacting them financially and in some cases destroying their reputation as clients fear the security of their information following a serious attack. In terms of governments, a destruction attack can plunge the systems into chaos. It can take some amount

43

of time for an organization to recover fully from the most severe destruction attack, as is the objective for the hacker.

Disinformation - Equally devastating can be that of disinformation. This involved spreading credibility destroying rumours and information, having a severe impact on the target. The rumours that are launched may or may not be true however they can be equally devastating and can still have long term effects on the organization or nation involved. Once these attacks are carried out, damage control can be quite challenging as information can spread regardless of whether the infiltration is contained. Information can relate to certain scandals and claims of corruption which can tarnish the reputation of individuals within the organization or the organization itself, leading to disruption of the order that has held the organization together.

Denial of Service - We have mentioned denial of service earlier in this book as it one of the most common and widely known forms of attack. In terms of cyberterrorism, DoS attacks occur with businesses and entities that have an online presence with the attack rendering the website or service useless at the time of the attack. These types of attacks can therefore cause immense issues in both the social and economic function of the business, causing organizations to suffer massive losses.

Defacement of Web Sites - While not as severe or damage, the defacement of a website can still have immense consequences for a business. Defacement of websites can involve websites to be changed completely, including a message from cyber terrorists for either propaganda or publicity purposes for them to achieve some type of cause. In other cases, hackers may cause the website to redirect to one in which they have established earlier which could also contain a message that they have devised to gain publicity and awareness of their propaganda or cause. These types of attacks have decreased in recent years as security measures have been heightened and hackers have a lower probability of access to web pages long enough to implement the changes and most major organizations effectively putting a stop to it.

Chapter Seven: Strategies to Combat Cyber Terrorist Threats

Implement strategic plans to counter cyber terrorist efforts will ensure that your organization has the means to combat any threats it may face. There are a number of strategies which a business can employee or in order to stay ahead and heighten their security capabilities in the face of a threat. These are:

Prosecuting Perpetrators

Many attacks can behind the wall of anonymity with many smaller organizations failing to pursue and prosecute the hackers responsible. While this can be a costly activity, there are some advantages in identifying and taking the attackers to court. This can be a shock to the cyber terrorist community and set the standard for which other organizations should conduct themselves in the wake of an attack. If the case is particularly high profile, the organization can benefit from the hard-line response with the prosecuted hackers being an example to the rest of the criminal organizations that are determined to wreak havoc on your business. This example set can send waves throughout the rest of the community and can lead to improvements in the investigation and prosecution process of criminal cyber terrorists. Therefore, is always in the best interest of the parties that have been affected by an attack to seek justice.

Develop New Security Practices

As an organization faces an attack, they will follow through in revaluating their security and any potential loopholes that could be exploited. This involves further testing such as the pen-testing we explored earlier as a means of finding weaknesses and vulnerabilities and employing new security means to combat these. These activities require cooperation and coordinated efforts amongst all departments within an organization to ensure maximum effectiveness. Corporations should review international standard guidelines for security information to detail the steps that should be taken in order to secure organizations in terms of information security. As organizations further develop their security capabilities, they are able to adapt and modify the standard guidelines to comply with their own operations and needs to achieve the best results.

Take a Proactive Approach

It is important for both corporations and the general public to take a proactive approach as the threat from cyber terrorism becomes more sophisticated and targeted. This involves keeping up to date with the latest information within the cyber security sphere such as threats, vulnerabilities and noteworthy incidents as they will allow security professionals to gain a deeper insight into how these components could affect their organizations. From there they are able to develop and implement stronger security measures thereby reducing the opportunities for hackers to exploit for cyber-attacks.

Organizations should constantly be on the forefront of cyber security having a multi-level security infrastructure in order to protect valuable data and user's private information. All activities that are critical in nature should have security audits frequently to ensure all policies and procedures relating to security are adhered to. Security should be treated as an ongoing and continuous process rather than an aftermath of the consequences of an attack.

Deploy Vital Security Applications

There are many tools available for security professionals to protect their networks and they can provide a significant benefit to the job at hand. These applications involve firewalls, IDS, as well as anti-virus software that can ensure better protections against potential hackers. Using these security systems, security personnel are able to record, monitor and report any suspicious activities that can indicate the system is at risk. The applications are able to streamline the process, making the job far more efficient and effective. Utilizing these types of tools ensures that security personnel are assisted with the latest in prevention technology and have a greater probability of combating attackers.

Establish Business Disaster Recovery Plans

In the event that an attack does occur, all businesses should have a worst-case scenario contingency plan in place to ensure that processes and operations are brought back to normally as soon as possible. Without such plans, the consequences can be disastrous leading to a loss in revenue and reputation on behalf of the business. Once these plans have been devised, they should be rehearsed regularly in order to test their effectiveness and also provide staff with training in the event of an attack.

These plans should be comprised of two main components, these being, repair and restoration. From the perspective of repair, the attacking force should be neutralised as soon as possible with the objective to return operations to normalcy and have all functions up and running. The restoration element is geared towards having pre-specified arrangements with hardware, software as well as a network comprised of service vendors, emergency services and public utilities on hand to assist in the restoration process.

Cooperation with Other Firms

Your organization would not be alone in dealing with the aftermath of a cyber-attack. Many organizations exist in order to deal with cyber terrorism threats both public and private. These groups can go a long way in helping with issues relating to cyber terrorism such as improving the security within your organization, helping devise and implement disaster recovery plans and further discuss how you can deal with threats in the future and what this means for the wider community. Having this extended network available to you will enhance your efforts in resisting cyber-attacks as well as having a role in discussing other emerging threats and protecting organizations facing these same threats.

Increasing Security Awareness

It is important not to become complacent in times where security threats are prevalent and this requires an increase in awareness with all issues relating to cyber security. Having your organization become an authority in raising awareness within the community will help educate other organizations in how they can defend themselves against attacks and strengthen their own security which in turn will damage the cyberterrorist community as they face a stronger resistance. You can also raise awareness within your own organization through security training programs which will help all employees equip themselves with the right skillset to combat threats that could arise through their own negligence and will also help them be more alert in times when threats could be present.

Chapter Eight: Basic Guide to Hacking

Now that you have a good understanding of hacking concepts and what is involved in the penetration of a system as well as how you can turn hacking into a career, we want to get into the heart of the action and learning how to carry out an effective attack. This is for demonstration purposes to help strengthen your knowledge and ideally stem further education. If you are still unsure on the basics of hacking, have a read through and study this book thoroughly as we will be going through this step by step guide with the assumption that you have a solid grasp of the topics of hacking and computer security and we wouldn't want you to get lost along the way.

Before you do get started, you will need to utilize a tool to help with the pen-test. For this example, we will be using Metasploit, an open source tool which has a number of functions which pen-testers and black hat hackers alike will find incredibly useful. The tool has a database filled with a large number of known exploits which can be picked up during the vulnerability test by the variety of scanners. Metasploit is one of the more popular pen-testing software applications and as an open source program, there is a large community which you can interact with in case you have any questions or concerns.

For the purpose of this example, we will be hacking into a virtual machine as this is a great way to practice and scan for weaknesses without actually breaking into an established machine. We will be scanning our virtual machine for exploits upon which we will then penetrate the system and extract the information we require. The virtual machine will also have limited access meaning it won't actually be accessible as easy to other people who may be scanning your network, leaving you in complete control. In order to create a virtual machine, we will be using VirtualBox, a software that allows you to establish a hacking lab in order to test your skills on a simulated machine. VirtualBox is another open source software that allows you to have access to the source code free of charge, allowing you to customise your build to your specifications.

Before continuing with your experiment ensure that the techniques and tools you use throughout this test are confined only to your machine and never used on other computers as this is not only illegal, it is also potentially dangerous. Even if you are simply learning how to carry out an attack for the purpose of your own education, if you are caught you can be prosecuted, and as you should have a good understanding from reading this book, this can be quite a serious crime and yes, it is possible to be caught. Keeping this in mind, let us go through with our virtual pen-test.

Initial Preparation

The first step toward setting up your environment is creating virtual machine to run on VirtualBox. You will need two machines, a target and a victim. You are able to download these online, they will come with files that we can extract as well as vulnerabilities to exploit. Once you have the files in place, extract them and create a new machine on VirtualBox and choose the type of machine you will be using. From there you decide how much RAM your machine will be running with, this isn't too important so selecting a small amount won't affect your test, 512MB is a good starting point.

Your next task is then to select a hard disk by checking the Use an Existing Disk option. You are able to click on the folder option and select the appropriate file that you had extracted from your download files and once that is all done, click create and your virtual machine and you are ready to move onto the next step.

Creating a Network

In order to access your machine, you will need to establish a virtual network. This is to keep your machine safe from existing threats outside your control. You are able to do this through VirtualBox by going through File > Preferences > Network > Host Only Network. Once you click the plus sign, you are able to add a new entry which will be your virtual network. Now is time to add your virtual machine to the virtual network. You are able to do this by selecting your virtual machine and clicking settings from the menu. From there you will see the network tab which will allow you to click 'Attacked to' from and Host-Only Adaptor from the drop-down menu.

Attacking Tools

Now that your network and machine have been set up it is time to acquire the tools to launch your attack. In this example, we will be using Kali as it is simple to set up and you can also run it live in a virtual machine. Once you have downloaded Kali as an ISO file, open VirtualBox and click Add to allow you to create another machine which will be your attacker. For your attacker, you want to allocate some more memory to the machine of around 2GB, if your machine has less than 4GB on the system, you may need to allocate less. You will not need to allocate any hard drive space, Kali is running live so check the box Do Not Add a Virtual Hard Drive. Once you are ready, hit create and your offending machine will be created. Ensure that you attach the machine to your network and change the adapter to host-holy. From here, you will start both machines and run Kali on your attack machine when prompted to add a bootable CD. You are then presented with the interface, and are ready to start scanning and gathering information from the Kali desktop interface.

Gathering Information

The next step in carrying out your attack is deciding upon your target. For the purpose of this experiment, we will be carrying out the attack on our victim server. In reality, this is a simple surface attack rather than focusing on the entire network that we had set up or the virtualization tools. From there it is time to gather information to discover the vulnerabilities that we will be exploiting. In order to do this, we will need to set this up in the software. This is where Metasploit will come into play as our framework for carrying out the pen-test, taking us through the process.

It is now time to begin collecting information. To do this, we must first we must initiate the services through Kali by entering:

"service postgresql start"

"service metasploit start"

Metasploit is best used through the console interface known as MSFConsole which is opened with

"Msfconsole"

Now you are ready to start your scan.

Scanning for Ports

In order to gather information on ports, you can use Nmap which is built into MSFconsole. In order to set this up, you will first need to enter the IP address of the target which you can find by typing in

"ifconfig"

This will then bring up information on the IP address, labelled inet addr within the eth0 block. The IP address should be similar to other machines found on your network. By running a scan of the IP address by using

Db_map -sS -A *TARGET IP ADDRESS*

You are able to have detailed list of all services running on the machine. From there you are able gather further information on each of the services to discover any vulnerabilities to exploit. Once you have found the weakest point, you are able to move into attack mode.

Exploitation

By enter services into MSFconsole, you are able to access the database of information on the services running on the machine. Once you have discovered a service that is particularly vulnerable, you are able to scan this service to assess points of weakness. This is done by typing

Search *service name*

Once you have done this, you will be provided a list of exploits which you can take advantage and can then tell MSFconsole to exploit the model. Once you have set the target, you simply need to type the command "run" for the program to work its magic and access the port. You will then be able to see what you are able to do once operating from the computer with a number of commands at your disposal with the permissions provided to you by the service. From here you are able to extract data as well as upload data depending on your objective.

Once you have accessed the machine, you will obviously want to ensure that you remained in control and fortunately Metasploit has a number of tools to assist.

Final Words

Having a deeper understanding of the meaning behind the word hacker can open up new doors for you not just within your career if you decide to explore IT security but also within your business and personal life as you become better equipped in dealing with external threats to your networks and systems. Before reading this book, you like many other people, may have had some misconceptions about what hacking actually means, who is behind it, why they do it, what they have to gain from it and what can be done to prevent them.

Now that you have reached the end of our book on hacking, you should have a much greater insight into the world of hacking including what it means to be an ethical hacker and how they operate. Knowing that an ethical hacker is also known as a white hat hacker, you also learnt the difference between white and black hat hackers, who are motivated by personal reasons whether that could be financial or ideological. You also gained some insight into the hackers that lie on the boundaries of ethics such as those known as grey hats and red hats as well the hacktivists that so often capture our awareness in the media.

We also explored the techniques used by hackers to attack your computer and what each of these attacks can do to a system, the seriousness behind them and the types of hackers that employ these tactics to achieve their motivations. Upon learning these techniques, you also learnt how it was possible to avoid becoming a target through precautions which can protect your system and the information contained on it.

We then moved onto the topic on penetration testing and how organizations are able to simulate attacks on their own systems in order to expose weaknesses and vulnerabilities that could be exploited by external hackers. We learnt the basic process of how a pen-test works and why it is performed. This gave us some insight into the world of ethical hackers and what their job is comprised of. Once learning this, we took a deeper look into careers in IT security, how the indri is moving and the qualifications that are widely recognised in the industry.

We then took a look at the other side of the coin into the world of cyber terrorism. We explored the reasoning's behind why terrorists carry out these attacks as well as how organizations are able to better equip themselves for dealing with these threats. In looking at each type of attack, we gained an understand how businesses need to be extra vigilant to avoid suffering losses both financial and intangible.

Towards the end of the book we walked through the basic setup of a pen-test and how it can be performed using a lab type scenario on a virtual machine. While this was just a brief cover of a pen-test, it hopefully spurred some curiosity for you to continue your education further and develop new skills in hacking. With the now solid understanding of hacking in your possession, it is worth exploring further certifications and courses that will allow you to get closer to a career in security as a white hat hacker and expressing your skills in a healthy environment or just to expand your knowledge and become more aware.

www.ingramcontent.com/pod-product-compliance
Lightning Source LLC
LaVergne TN
LVHW052314060326
832902LV00021B/3892